Books in this series

Animal Stories

for **6** year olds

Illustrated by
Atholl McDonald

Chosen by Helen Paiba

MACMILLAN CHILDREN'S BOOKS

First published 1999 by Macmillan Children's Books

This edition published 2017 by Macmillan Children's Books
an imprint of Pan Macmillan
20 New Wharf Road, London N1 9RR
Associated companies throughout the world
www.panmacmillan.com

ISBN 978-1-5098-3878-3

1 3 5 7 9 8 6 4 2

A CIP catalogue record for this book is available from
the British Library.

Typeset by SX Composing DTP, Rayleigh, Essex
Printed and bound by CPI Group (UK) Ltd, Croydon CR0 4YY

Contents

The Miserable Mouse

Dorothy Edwards

There was once a mouse who lived in a house with an old lady and an old gentleman. It wasn't a happy mouse, because it hadn't any friends. It wanted friends very much. It specially wanted to be friends with the old lady and gentleman it lived with, but it was no good.

They didn't like mice.

If the old lady even caught a

glimpse of it, she would shriek and jump on her chair, and that isn't the way to behave to a lonely mouse who wants to be friends, is it?

As for the old gentleman, he had just to see the merest flicker of a mousy whisker, and he would jump up with a roar and bang, bang, bang on the floor in such a way that he made it very clear he didn't want to be friendly either!

It was *such* a pity. It was such a nice brown clean beady-eyed mouse, with *such* a whippy tail, and such a friendly nature!

"I can't abide mousies," the old lady said. "Creeping, stealing

creatures is mousies! Always a-
eating and a-nibbling they be."

That wasn't true of *this* mouse
for a start. Of course, he had to eat
– everyone has to do that. But
Mousie only took crumbs and bits
from the floor that no one wanted
anyway. He never even dreamed of
stealing the large pieces of cheese
he saw on the mousetrap that the
old people left on the kitchen
floor!

"One mouse means many mice,"
the old gentleman said. "If we
don't rid ourselves of this one,
we'll be overrun!"

Which just showed that the old
gentleman didn't know much

about it. Our mouse was the only one in that house, and it takes two mice to be a father and a mother and make lots of little baby mice, doesn't it?

No, it was very dull for our mouse to be a mouse-on-his-own, especially as he knew the old people didn't like him. However, he thought he would be *very patient* and try to win them round. In the meantime, he made a little hole in the wainscot, which he used like a window, so that he could see the old people, although they couldn't see him. It was very interesting too. The old lady did lots of darning and mending, and the old gentleman looked at the television in the evening. Mousie couldn't understand this at all.

Up would go the old lady's arm with a thread of wool hanging from it, and the needle flashed and the thimble glittered in the lamplight. It was very hard for Mousie to make out what she was doing. For mice don't wear the sort of clothes that need mending!

And as for the old gentleman and his box of jumping lights! Well, if they'd only be friendly they would soon find that Mouse was more interesting than that old thing. Mouse could whisk for them and frisk for them, and lick his paws and jump for them. Oh, if only they would *take* to him! So Mouse was lonely. And it might have gone on like that for ever. Mouse might even have gone back to live with his relations, if it hadn't been for a careless man in a television studio, who fell over a long wire and stopped all the television sets in all the people's houses from showing the programme the old gentleman was looking at.

It was a cowboy film, and the nasty man in the film was just creeping up behind the good nice cowboy when the picture disappeared, so the old gentleman was very cross.

Because he *was* cross, he jumped up quickly, and that made the old lady prick her finger with her darning needle. At the same time, she dropped her thimble, and it rolled across the floor, and dropped right through the hole that was the mouse's front door. The clumsy television man soon put the film back again, so that the old gentleman could see the nice cowboys and nasty men fighting, but the poor old lady was quite lost without her thimble – she couldn't finish her mending!

She hunted and hunted for it, but she couldn't find it. She sighed and fidgeted so much that she upset the old gentleman. How could he look at cowboys when the old lady was crawling round his chair? So he got up and helped her.

But oh dear, the thimble was lost!

"Oh deary me!" said the old lady. "Now I can't finish my mending. I'm lost without my mending, that I be." And she sat down in her chair and sighed and sighed.

And that was the mouse's chance!

Quick as a flash, he darted out of his hole and into the room. He came with a jingle-jingle noise and they both saw him at once. He was jingle-jingling because he was

balancing that thimble on his
right-hand front whisker, and as it
jiggled about it jangled like a little
bell. The little mouse stood quite
still at the old lady's feet, and sat
himself up just like a little
begging dog, and twiddled his
whisker with the thimble on it
again and again.

"Bless the little creature," said the old lady. "It's brought me thimble, so 'tas. The pretty dear then! Look, Dad, did you ever?"

The old gentleman stared and stared. "W-e-ll I'll be blowed," he said.

The old lady stooped down, and gently, gently she took the thimble from Mousie's whisker, and put it back onto her finger.

"Don't go, Mousie," she said. "I'm just going to get our evening cocoa and biscuits. You might as well stay and have a bite to eat with us."

And she went off to the kitchen at once, and very soon she came back, not only with the cocoa and biscuits, but a whole saucerful of tasty bits from the larder.

The mouse ate them very daintily, and washed his whiskers afterwards to show that he was a clean, good-mannered creature.

"When you've finished that-there blow-out," said the old gentleman, "you can come and watch the tallyvision along o'me."

And that was just what the mouse wanted. At last he had a chance to see properly what it was that the old man watched in the evening.

He climbed happily onto the old gentleman's knee, and sat twirling his whiskers and looking at the

cowboys, and although he couldn't make head or tail of it, he was happy as happy. From time to time the old lady looked across and smiled at him, and from time to time the old gentleman stroked his soft grey fur.

Now, he was more than a friend. He was one of the family!

A Lion in the Meadow

Margaret Mahy

The little boy said,
      "Mother, there is a lion in
the meadow."
   The mother said,
   "Nonsense, little boy."
   The little boy said,
   "Mother, there is a big yellow
lion in the meadow."
   The mother said,
   "Nonsense, little boy."
   The little boy said,

"Mother, there is a big, roaring, yellow, whiskery lion in the meadow!"

The mother said,

"Little boy, are are making up stories again. There is nothing in the meadow but grass and trees. Go into the meadow and see for yourself."

The little boy said,

"Mother, I'm scared to go into the meadow because of the lion which is there."

The mother said,

"Little boy, you are making up stories – so I will make up a story, too . . . Do you see this matchbox? Take it out into the meadow and open it. In it will be a tiny dragon. The tiny dragon will grow into a big dragon. It will chase the lion away."

The little boy took the matchbox and went away. The mother went on peeling the potatoes.

Suddenly the door opened.

In rushed a big, roaring, yellow, whiskery lion.

"Hide me!" it said. "A dragon is after me!"

The lion hid in the broom cupboard.

Then the little boy came running in.

"Mother," he said. "That dragon grew too big. There is no lion in the meadow now. There is a *dragon* in the meadow."

The little boy hid in the broom cupboard too.

"You should have left me alone," said the lion. "I eat only apples."

"But there wasn't a real dragon," said the mother. "It was just a story I made up."

"It turned out to be true after all," said the little boy. "You should have looked in the matchbox first."

"That is how it is," said the lion. "Some stories are true, and some aren't . . . But I have an idea. We will go and play in the meadow on the other side of the house. There is no dragon there."

"I am glad we are friends now," said the little boy.

The little boy and the big, roaring, yellow, whiskery lion went to play in the other meadow. The dragon stayed where he was, and nobody minded.

The mother never ever made up a story again.

Koala's Walkabout

Anita Hewett

Koala sat in the crook of a tree under a roof of leaves, and he said:

"It's a pity to stay at home all day, when the sun is shining so brightly outside. So I think I'll go for a walkabout. I know I'm rather slow on my legs, but if I start early and don't waste time, I can get to the Blue Misty Mountains and back."

Off went Koala between the trees, shuffling along on his slow furry legs. Some of his friends would have stopped to talk, but Koala said: "No. I can't spare the time. I must hurry, hurry, all the way, or I shan't get back to my tree tonight."

At the edge of the forest Koala saw Python Snake.

Python had tied himself into a knot. The more he tried to untangle himself, the tighter the knot became and the worse his temper got.

He wriggled and pulled in the wrong directions until it seemed he would burst with rage.

19

"Poor old Python is tangled," said Koala. "Who will help him? *I* can't stop."

Koala walked on, but his steps were slow.

"How should *I* feel?" he said to himself. "How should *I* feel, with a knot in my middle?"

And he turned around and hurried back to poor old struggling Python Snake.

"Do as I say," he told the snake. "Do as I say and I'll get you untangled."

He looked at the knot from the left and the right.

Then he waved a paw in the air and said:

"That way! Wriggle a bit to the left. Yes, a bit more. That's it. That's the way."

Then he waved his other paw, and said:

"Now, pull back. But very slowly. Back! And wriggle a bit to the right."

21

Koala looked at the knot again.

"It's looser," he said. "You're getting untangled. Wriggle once more to the right, and you're straight."

Python lay long and straight on the ground.

"I feel so comfortable," he said. "Thanks for the help." And he glided away.

Koala's short legs went stumping along, trying to make up the time he had lost. But the Blue Misty Mountains were far away when he came at last to the tangled scrubland. And then he saw Cassowary Bird, pushing and kicking his way through the scrub.

"Bother! Oh dear!" said the big black bird. "Where did I put it? I really must find it."

"What have you lost?" called Koala, as he stumped on his way across the scrub.

Cassowary called: "An egg! Mrs Cassowary's egg! I promised to watch the egg, and I've lost it. At least, I haven't really lost it, but I just can't find it!"

And he got very angry and kicked at a bush.

"Cassowary is worried," said Koala. "But I really can't spare the time to help him. I must hurry, hurry, as fast as I can, if I want to get to the mountains and back."

23

On he went, but his steps were slow.

"I don't lay eggs myself," he said. "But how should I feel if I did, and I lost one?"

He turned around and hurried back to worried Cassowary Bird.

"I think you should look very slowly and carefully," he said. "You look *that* way, and I'll look *this* way."

Cassowary moved to the left, stepping gently, carefully searching. Koala moved to the right, very slowly, patting the grasses with careful paws.

"Look!" he shouted at last. "What's this?"

He raised two paws above his head, and there between them, large and green, was Mrs Cassowary's egg.

"Put it down on the grass," said the bird. "Ah! It's a beautiful egg, don't you think? Thank you for finding it, Koala."

The sun was already high in the sky as Koala hurried towards the rockland. The mountains were still a long way off, and Koala's paws were sore on the rocks. He was glad when he came to some tussocky grass.

"Now I can hurry, hurry," he said.

Then he saw Bat. And Bat was

25

frightened. His claw was caught in a tangle of grass, and he flapped and pulled as he tried to get free.

"I don't like the sun; it burns me," he wailed. "I want to go home to my cool dark cave, but I'm caught, and I'm burning. I think I shall die."

Koala turned his face to the mountains.

"If I stop to help him my day will be spoiled. I'm very late already," he said.

On he went, but his steps were slow.

"How should *I* feel?" he said to himself. "How should *I* feel, caught in a tussock, burnt by the sun and a long way from home?"

And he turned around, and went back to Bat.

"Poor little Bat. Don't be frightened," he said. "I'll help you. You needn't be scared any more."

He put his paws beneath Bat's wings, and gently pulled him away from the tussock.

"Thank you," said Bat, as he fluttered away. "Now I can go to my cave until night comes."

Koala did not stop again, and at last he came to the Blue Misty Mountains. He rested, gazing with solemn eyes, warm and happy inside with gladness.

"So I *have* seen the Blue Misty

Mountains," he said.

Then he turned around, and set off for home.

He made his aching legs move fast, because dangerous things could happen at night to a little animal who was all by himself.

When he reached the edge of the rocky land, he knew he must rest, just for a minute. Most of the rocks were sharp and rough, so Koala was pleased when he saw a round shape that looked smooth and comfortable for sitting. He sighed as he rested his aching legs.

"I shall soon feel better again," he said. "This rock makes a very good seat for a koala."

28

The rock rose up on four strong legs, and marched away, tipping and tilting, with Koala clinging to its back. It was *not* a rock, it was Great Green Turtle.

"Help!" cried Koala. "Stop, Green Turtle. Let me get down. I shall fall on the rocks. I shall hurt myself dreadfully. Stop, Turtle, stop!"

But on went Turtle, tipping and tilting, while Koala clung to his slippery back.

Suddenly, out of the scrub glided Python, stretching his body in front of Turtle, long and straight, a great snake wall. And Turtle stopped. He could go no farther.

Koala clambered from Turtle's back, safe on his own four legs again.

"Thank you, Python Snake," he said, and on he went across the scrub, with wobbly, aching, hurrying legs. There were strange dark shapes in the scrub at night.

Suddenly Koala shivered with fright. From behind a bush came a strange new sound, a yelping, howling, horrible sound. And after the sound came two gleaming eyes. Wild Dog Dingo was on the prowl.

Koala turned around and ran. And after him, snapping sharp teeth, came Dingo.

Out of the scrub came

30

Cassowary, kicking his legs and stretching his neck. He ran at howling Dingo Dog, and Dingo went yelping into the darkness.

Koala sat down for a very short rest.

"Thank you, Cassowary," he said, and on he went, into the forest.

Koala's legs were dreadfully tired. He could hardly lift them off the ground.

"*That's* not my tree, I know," he said. "Neither is that, nor that, nor that. I shall *never* find my tree," he said.

Out of the darkness came little black Bat, who liked to do his flying at night. *He* knew the trees in the moonlight.

He fluttered over Koala's head, then he glided away through the cool dark night. Koala followed, while black Bat swooped and fluttered ahead, leading the way through the strange dark forest.

Then all at once it was *not* a

strange forest. It was Koala's forest, a friendly place. He saw his own strong sheltering tree, and he knew he was safe, and home again.

"Oh!" said Koala. "Thank you, Bat."

He climbed up into the crook of his tree, and curled himself into a sleepy bundle.

But before he closed his eyes he said:

"I know I'm rather slow on my legs, but I *did* see the mountains. I'm glad."

Then he slept.

The Excitement of Being Ernest

Dick King-Smith

The first thing that struck you about Ernest was his colour. If you had to put a name to it, you would say "honey" – not that pale waxy honey that needs a knife to get it out of a jar, but the darker, richer, runny stuff that drips all over the tablecloth if you don't wind the spoon round it properly.

That was the colour of Ernest's coat, and the second thing about him that was remarkable was the amount of coat he carried. He was very hairy. Body, legs, tail, all had their fair share of that runny-honey-coloured hair, but it was Ernest's face that was his fortune, with its fine beard and moustaches framed by shortish, droopy ears. From under bushy eyebrows, Ernest looked out upon the world and found it good. Only one thing bothered him. He did not know what kind of dog he was.

It should have been simple, of course, to find out. There were a number of other dogs living in the village who could presumably have told him, but somehow Ernest had never plucked up the courage to ask. To begin with, the other dogs all looked so posh. They were all of different breeds, but each one appeared so obviously well-bred, so self-assured, so upper class, that Ernest had always hesitated to approach them, least of all with a daft question like, "Excuse me. I wonder if you could tell me what sort of dog I am?"

For that matter, he thought to himself one day, *I don't even know what sort of dogs they are*, and then it occurred to him that would be a much more sensible question to ask and could lead perhaps to the kind of conversation about breeds in general where one of them might say, "I'm a Thingummytite, and you, I see, are a Wotchermecallum."

So after he had helped to get the cows in for morning milking on the farm where he lived, Ernest trotted up to the village to the gateway of the Manor House – an imposing entrance flanked by fine pillars – and peered in under his bushy eyebrows. Standing in the drive was the Manor House dog. Ernest lifted his leg politely on one of the fine stone pillars, and called out, "Excuse me! I wonder if you could tell me what sort of dog you are?"

"Ich bin ein German Short-haired Pointer," said the Manor House dog, "If dot is any business of yours."

"Oh," said Ernest. "I'm not one of those."

He waited expectantly to be told what he was.

"Dot," said the German Short-haired Pointer pointedly, "is as plain as der nose on your face," and he turned his back and walked away.

Ernest went on to the Vicarage, and saw, through the wicket-gate, the Vicar's dog lying on the lawn.

"Excuse me," said Ernest, lifting his leg politely on the wicket-gate, "I wonder if you could tell me what sort of dog you are?"

"Nom d'un chien!" said the Vicar's dog. "Je suis un French Bulldog."

"Oh," said Ernest. "I'm not one of those."

The French Bulldog snorted, and though Ernest waited hopefully for a while, it said nothing more, so he walked down the road till he came to the pub.

The publican's dog was very large indeed, and Ernest thought it best to keep some distance away. He lifted his leg discreetly on an empty beer barrel and shouted across the pub car park, "Excuse me! I wonder if you could tell me what sort of dog you are?"

"Oi'm an Irish Wolfhound," said the publican's dog in a deep, rumbly voice.

"Oh," said Ernest. "I'm not one of those."

"Bedad you're not," said the Irish Wolfhound. "Shall Oi be after tellin' yez what sort of a dog ye are?"

"Oh, yes please," said Ernest eagerly.

"Sure ye're a misbegotten hairy mess," said the Irish Wolfhound, "and it's stinking of cow-muck ye are. Now bate it, if ye know what's good for you."

Ernest beat it. But he wasn't beaten.

He paid a call on a number of houses in the village street,

41

repeating his polite enquiry and receiving answers of varying degrees of rudeness from a Tibetan Terrier, an American Cocker Spaniel, a Finnish Spitz and a Chinese Crested Dog. But none of them volunteered any information as to what kind of animal he himself was.

There was one house left, by the junction of the road with the lane that led back to the farm, and standing outside it was a dog that Ernest had never seen before in the neighbourhood. It looked friendly and wagged its long, plumy tail as Ernest left his customary calling card on the gate.

"Hullo," he said. "I haven't seen you before."

"We've only just moved in," said the friendly stranger. "You're the first dog I've met here, actually. Are there a lot in the village?"

"Yes."

"Decent bunch?"

Ernest considered how best to answer this.

"They're all very well-bred," he said. "I imagine they've got pedigrees as long as your tail," he added, "like you have, I suppose?"

"Well, yes, you could say that," replied the other. "For what it's worth."

Ernest sighed. *I'll give it one more go*, he thought.

"Straight question," he said. "What sort of dog are you?"

"Straight answer, English Setter – well, at least on my mother's side."

"English?" said Ernest delightedly. "That makes a change."

"How do you mean?"

"Why, the rest of them are Chinese, German, Tibetan, Irish, American, Finnish – there's no end to the list."

"Really? No, no, I'm as English as you are."

"Ah," said Ernest carefully.

"Then you know what sort of dog I am?"

"Of course," said the Setter. "You're a Gloucestershire Cow-dog."

The hair over Ernest's face prevented the Setter from seeing the changing expression that flitted across it, first of astonishment, then of excitement, and finally a studied look of smug satisfaction.

"Ah," said Ernest. "You knew. Not many do."

"My dear chap," said the Setter. "You amaze me. I should have thought any dog would have recognized a Gloucestershire Cow-dog immediately."

"Really?" said Ernest. "Well, I suppose any English dog would."

"Yes, that must be it. Anyway you'll be able to compete with all these pedigree chaps next week."

"Why, what's happening next week?"

"It's the Village Fête."

"Oh, I don't go to that sort of thing," said Ernest. "I've got too much work to do with the cows."

"Quite. But this year there's a new attraction apparently. They've just put the posters up. Haven't you seen?"

"Didn't notice," said Ernest.

"Well, there's one stuck on our wall. Come and have a look."

46

And this is what they saw.

VILLAGE FÊTE
SATURDAY JUNE 15th
BY KIND PERMISSION
IN THE GROUNDS OF THE
MANOR HOUSE

Skittle Alley
Coconut Shy
Cake Stall
Jam and Preserve Stall
White Elephant Stall
Hoopla
Wellie-throwing Competition
Guess the Weight of the Pig
Grand Dog Show

"But that's no good," said Ernest. "With all the pedigree dogs in the village, the judge will never look twice at me."

"But that's no good," said Sally. "With all the pedigree dogs in the village, the judge will never look twice at Ernest." Sally was the farmer's daughter, and she was looking at another of the notices, tacked on the farm gate.

"Oh, I don't know," said her father. "You might be surprised. Have a go. It's only a bit of fun. You'll have to clean him up a bit, mind."

So when the great day dawned,

Ernest ran to Sally's whistle after morning milking and found himself, to his surprise and disgust, required to stand in an old tin bath and be soaked and lathered and scrubbed and hosed, and then blow-dried with Sally's mother's electric drier plugged into a power point in the dairy.

"He looks a treat," said the farmer and his wife when Sally had finished combing out that long, honey-coloured coat. And he did.

Indeed, when they all arrived at the Fête, a number of people had difficulty in recognizing Ernest without his usual covering of

49

cow-muck. But the dogs weren't fooled. Ernest heard them talking among themselves as the competitors began to gather for the Dog Show, and their comments made his head drop and his tail droop.

"Well, I'll be goshdarned!" said the American Cocker Spaniel to the Tibetan Terrier. "Will ya look at that mutt! Kinda tough to have to share a show-ring with no-account trash like that."

And, turning to the Finnish Spitz, "Velly distlessing," said the Chinese Crested Dog. "No pediglee."

"Ma foi!" said the French

Bulldog to the Irish Wolfhound. "Regardez zis 'airy creature! 'E is, 'ow you say, mongrel?"

"Begorrah, it's the truth ye're spakin," said the Irish Wolfhound in his deep, rumbly voice, "and it's stinking of soap powder he is."

As for the German Short-haired Pointer, he made sure, seeing that he was host for the day, that his comment on Ernest's arrival on the croquet lawn (which was the show-ring) was heard by all.

"Velcome to der Manor, ladies and gentlemen," he said to the other dogs. "May der best-bred dog vin." And he turned his back on Ernest in a very pointed way.

"Don't let them get you down, old chap," said a voice in Ernest's ear, and there, standing next to him, was the friendly Setter, long plumy tail wagging.

"Oh, hullo," said Ernest in a doleful voice. "Nice to see you. I hope you win, anyway. I haven't got a chance."

"Oh, I don't know," said the Setter. "You might be surprised. Have a go. It's only a bit of fun." he lowered his voice. "Take a tip though, old chap. Don't lift your leg. It's not done."

Suddenly Ernest felt much happier. He gave himself a good shake, and then when they all began to parade around the ring, he stepped out smartly at Sally's side, his long (clean) honey-coloured coat shining in the summer sunshine.

The judge examined each entry in turn, looking in their mouths, feeling their legs and their backs, studying them from all angles, and making them walk up and down, just as though it was a class in a Championship Show.

When her turn came, he said to Sally, "What's your dog called?"

"Ernest."

From under bushy eyebrows, Ernest looked out upon the judge.

"Hullo, Ernest," the judge said, and then hesitated, because there was one thing that bothered him. He did not know what kind of dog Ernest was.

"You don't see many of these," he said to Sally.

"Oh yes you do. There are lots about."

"Lots of . . . ?"

"Gloucestershire Cow-dogs."

"Of course, of course," said the judge.

When he had carefully examined all the entries, he made them walk round once more, and then he called out the lady of the Manor with her German Short-haired

Pointer. When they came eagerly forward, trying not to look too smug, he said, "I've finished with you, thank you."

And he called out, one after another, the Chinese Crested Dog and the Tibetan Terrier and the American Cocker Spaniel and the French Bulldog and the Irish Wolfhound and, to finish with, the Finnish Spitz, and said to each in turn, "I've finished with you, thank you."

Until the only dogs left on the croquet lawn were the Setter and Ernest.

And the judge looked thoughtfully at both of them for

quite a time before he straightened up and spoke to the owner of the Setter.

"A very close thing," he said, "but I'm giving the first prize to the Gloucestershire Cow-dog," and he walked across to the Vicar, whose job it was to make all the announcements on the public address system.

"Well done, old boy," said the Setter. "It couldn't have happened to a nicer chap."

"But I don't understand," said Ernest. "How could I have won? Against all you aristocratic fellows that are registered with the Kennel Club, and have lots of champions in your pedigrees?"

"Listen," said the Setter as the tannoy began to crackle and the voice of the Vicar boomed across the gardens of the Manor House.

"Ladies and gentlemen! We have the result of our Grand Dog Show! It's not quite like Crufts, ha, ha – we do things a bit differently down here – and in our Show there has been only one class, for The Most Lovable Dog. And the winner is . . . Ernest, the Gloucestershire Cow-dog!"

And Sally gave Ernest a big hug, and the judge gave Sally a little cup, and the Setter wagged his plumy tail like mad, and everybody clapped like billy-o, and Ernest barked and barked so loudly that he must have been heard by nearly every cow in Gloucestershire.

Oh, the excitement of being Ernest!

Snake on the Bus

Hazel Townson

It was Barney's birthday, though he still had to go to school. He opened his presents and cards at breakfast and collected quite a lot of money as well as some interesting parcels.

"One more present still to come," said Dad mysteriously. "You can have it tonight."

Barney took his birthday money to school and spent it on a snake;

a real, live snake.

Well, his parents had said he could buy what he wanted with the money, and he'd had his eye on this snake for weeks in the window of the pet shop next door to school. Its name was Sneaky. Now Sneaky was curled in a box on Barney's lap on the back seat of the school bus, going home. Would there be trouble when they arrived? Barney hoped not, but he could not help feeling just a little bit worried, all the same.

On the seat next to Barney his friend Nina was having her hair pulled by Mike the bully. Mike was leaning over from the seat in front, dragging Nina's head towards him.

"Ow! That hurts!" yelled Nina, who was only half the size of Mike.

"Give us your chocolate and I'll stop," said Mike.

"Never!" screeched Nina. She had bought the chocolate for her brother, who was laid up at home with a broken leg.

"We'll see about that!" shouted Mike, pulling so hard that he dragged Nina right off the seat. There was a crash and a cry, followed by a scuffle as Mike leapt from his seat and tried to snatch the chocolate from Nina's hand.

Barney wasn't having that! He

jumped up, eager to help his friend. But in his excitement he forgot about Sneaky. The cardboard box slid off Barney's lap the lid flew off the box and Sneaky slithered out, making straight for Mike's ankles.

"Help! A snake!" Mike hollered, fleeing down the aisle.

"What's going on back there?" yelled Tom, the school bus driver. "Any trouble and you'll all be sorry!"

Tom had been driving the school bus for years, and did not intend to put up with any nonsense.

"There's a snake on the bus, honest!" Mike went on. "It's after me! It's just gone under that seat."

Most of the children knew about Barney's snake, for he had let them peep into the box at the bus stop. But none of them liked Mike the bully, so they all kept Barney's secret to themselves.

"I can't see any snake, can you?" they asked one another.

"He's making it up to frighten us."

"Just the sort of thing he *would* do!"

"Don't take any notice of him, Tom!"

They were so convincing that even Mike began to wonder if he had imagined the snake. He sat down again, keeping a wary eye on the bus floor all the same.

Mike lived nearest to school so he was always first to get off the bus. Today he was glad when the bus reached his stop. He flew to the door, leapt down the steps and bolted along the pavement as fast as he could go. He did not notice that Sneaky had also made a quick exit from the bus and had slithered through the gateway of a much overgrown and tangled garden.

The children in the front seats noticed, though. They began to shout to Tom to wait a minute because the snake had escaped.

"You just said there *was* no

snake!" Tom retorted crossly as he drove off. "I don't know what you kids are up to, but the next one to mention a snake gets reported to the head teacher tomorrow."

Barney was really upset. He ran down the aisle, wanting to get off the bus to go and look for Sneaky, but Tom would not let him.

"I'm responsible for seeing you safe home," said Tom, ordering Barney back to his seat.

It was a desolate homecoming, not a bit like a birthday. Barney walked in with his empty box.

"What's that?" asked his mother, and the whole sad story came tumbling out. It no longer mattered whether his parents would *mind* having a snake, as there was not going to be one after all.

To Barney's hurt surprise, instead of consoling him his mother began to smile. But he soon found out why, for when Dad came home a little while later he was carrying a huge tank containing – a snake!

"Your belated birthday present," grinned Dad. "We knew you wanted a snake, but I couldn't collect it until this afternoon."

Great! Barney could not help being pleased. "But what about Sneaky?"

"Jump in the car and show me the garden where your friends said Sneaky had gone," Dad decided.

They drove to the garden at once – and there Sneaky was, curled up sleepily in the long grass. Dad had a word with the owners of the house, who were only too glad to let him take Sneaky away. Barney put Sneaky back into his box, which he had brought with him hopefully, and they drove back home.

"Now you've got a playmate as well," Barney told his pet. "Just wait till Mike the bully hears about that!"

Never Trust a Pelican

A Story from Thailand

Naomi Adler

Many, many miles away there is a land of great beauty, where the people dance and sing the animal stories they have heard told, over and over again, by the village storyteller.

Many moons ago, there was in this land a very beautiful lake. It was surrounded by a deep, green forest and high mountains. A mighty river flowed into the lake, a river that came from a spring in the mountains, a river that journeyed far and wide over rocks and cascades, tumbling down waterfalls and winding its way until it reached the beautiful lake. The lake was full of life, full of plants, full of frogs and fish and even crabs.

Now there was also a lone pelican living alongside the lake. This pelican had lost his family and friends long, long ago. Now he was old and feeble and lived by the side of the lake all alone. Every day the pelican waded his way into the deeper water to catch the little juicy fish that swam by. But now that he was getting older and weaker he was finding it more and more difficult to catch the little playful fish. Most days the pelican went home hungry and miserable. He realized that he would soon starve to death if he didn't catch a single fish.

One bright day, the pelican was staring into the water wondering how he could make a plan to catch the fish without so much effort. Suddenly, upon seeing his own reflection in the water and recognizing what a wonderful and clever bird he was, a tremendous and most cunning idea came into his head.

"Yes!" he laughed out loud. "That's exactly what I will do!"

So the pelican put his plan into action.

The pelican stood by the side of the lake looking very sad indeed. He wasn't even tempted to try and catch the fish swimming past him. The creatures of the lake noticed how very sad the pelican was and they began to wonder what had happened to him.

The old crab, who was the wisest and most courageous of all the creatures of the lake, came up to the pelican and asked, "Why are you so sad, Pelican?"

"Oh dear, oh dear, oh dear me," replied the pelican. "There are such bad times coming to this lake, such great danger is coming to all of us animals."

"Dear me! Dear me! What is this great danger? Please tell me," said the crab.

"Indeed, we are all in very great danger," proclaimed the pelican. "Soon no more water will flow down from the mountain. The river will cease to tumble over the rocks and the lake will dry up to nothing. We will all die and vanish."

The crab was most alarmed and passed on the news to the fish and frogs. The fish were even more alarmed. After all, the pelican could fly off and the frogs could hop off and the crabs could creep off sideways. But what about the fish? They could neither fly, hop nor creep.

The poor fish panicked and swam round and round in circles wailing, "What will become of us and our little babies, what will become of us?"

The largest and fattest of all the fish then came up to the pelican and said, "Dear Pelican, you have indeed given us very bad news. But you are a clever chap; please tell us how we can save ourselves."

The pelican replied, "I am only a
bird, but I may be able to help you
in a very small way." He
continued, "There is another lake,
even larger and more beautiful, a
little distance from here. This lake
has a never-ending spring in the
centre of it. The water there will
never stop, the lake will never dry

up. I can take you there if you wish."

"You are indeed a good friend," said the fish. "You can save us. Please take us in your beak to that other lake."

"It is an extremely difficult task," said the pelican. "But I will do my best."

When they heard this all the fish began to cry out, "Take me first, take me first."

"Be patient," said the pelican. "I can only carry a few of you at a time. But I shall make as many journeys as I need to. I am very old and feeble now and I may need to have lots of rests between journeys so this task may take some time. But I do promise to save you all."

The pelican chose the plumpest of the fish, seized them in his beak and flew off to the other side of the deep, green forest. He landed on a large rock and there in peace and quiet he ate them all up, leaving only a few fins and bones on the rock.

He then returned for more. He only had to say, "Who is next?"

"Me, me, take me," called the fish.

So he seized more fish and flew them to the rock where he gobbled them up too.

Whenever the pelican was full, he rested and slept in the lovely, warm sun. Whenever the pelican was hungry, he flew back to the lake where more fish were eagerly awaiting their turn to be rescued.

Now, one day, the oldest and wisest crab began to wonder about this great danger. He was very different from the fish, you see; he had travelled a great deal and had seen many things and had learnt many things too. He began to realize that if the water was still flowing so strongly from the mountain then the story of the drought was surely not true. In that case the pelican could not be trusted.

The oldest and wisest crab decided to find out what was going on. So the very next day when the pelican arrived at the lake and called out, "Who is next?", the crab said,

"Take me, take me, dear Pelican."

The pelican was delighted; he was getting rather bored with so many fish. He suddenly developed a taste for crab meat and readily agreed.

"I am at your service; come, I shall take you to the new lake."

The pelican seized the crab in

his beak and flew over the deep, green forest to the large rock on the other side.

The wise old crab looked down expecting to see a beautiful lake. But no, all he saw was a large rock covered with fins and bones. He knew at once what had happened.

The crab was afraid. He realized instantly that the pelican would land on the rock, kill him and eat him up. Just as he had done with all the fish. The crab thought and thought. What could he do to save himself and all the remaining fish in the lake?

All at once he seized the pelican round his neck with his strong pincers. The pelican struggled, flapped his wings in a panic and tried his utmost to rid himself of the crab. But the crab held tight, pressing harder and harder on the bird's neck. Soon the pelican fell to the ground like a heavy stone and that was the end of the pelican.

Slowly, the crab made his way back to the lake, creeping sideways, as crabs usually do, all the long journey back. When he finally reached the lake, the fish were very surprised to see him.

"Why have you come back? And where is the pelican?" they all cried out. The old crab then told them how the pelican had been cheating them and how he had put an end to the pelican . . .

From that day to this, frogs, fish and crabs have never made friends with pelicans.

Ursula on the Farm

Sheila Lavelle

Ursula had blue eyes and brown hair and a dimple in her cheek when she smiled. She looked just like an ordinary little girl.

But Ursula had a very special secret.

Ursula could turn herself into a bear.

She had found the spell in a book in the library. All she needed was a currant bun, filled with a mixture of porridge oats and honey.

A few magic words, and hey presto! Ursula would turn into a real, live bear.

Ursula had lots of fun being a bear. And turning back into herself again afterwards was simple.

A plate of beefburgers and chips did the trick, every single time.

One day, when Ursula was at school, Miss Plum came smiling into the classroom with a letter in her hand.

"Listen, children," she said. "This is from Mr Ford, the farmer.

We've all been invited to spend a day on his farm."

There was a lot of noise while everybody shouted "Hooray!" and "Whoopee!"

Ursula was very excited. She had never been to a farm before.

"Will there be animals?" she asked the teacher.

"Yes, Ursula," smiled Miss Plum. "There'll be cows and pigs, sheep and goats, ducks and hens, and maybe even some baby lambs."

Ursula ran home to tell Aunt Prudence all about it.

Aunt Prudence didn't know Ursula's secret. But she did know that Ursula was very fond of currant buns.

So when she packed Ursula's lunch bag on the day of the visit, she put in an extra-large one.

And she didn't forget Ursula's favourite filling of porridge oats and honey.

"Can I have a beefburger as well?" begged Ursula. "And a few chips?"

"Chips?" said Aunt Prudence in astonishment. "They'll get cold."

"I like cold chips," said Ursula. And she was very pleased when kind Aunt Prudence did as she asked. Now Ursula had everything she needed to turn into a bear and back again.

In the bus, everybody sang "Old Macdonald had a farm". Even Miss Plum joined in.

Ursula looked out of the window at the trees and the green fields.

Mr Ford was waiting for them at the farm gate, with a black and white sheepdog called Ben.

The children climbed out of the bus and gazed about them with round eyes.

Ben put his nose into Ursula's bag and sniffed at the beefburger.

"That's not for you," laughed Ursula.

"Come along, everybody," said the farmer. And he showed them all round the farm.

They saw the cows being milked in the sheds, and they fed the baby calves.

The boys helped the farmer's wife to give the pigs their bucket of mash.

There were sixteen pink piglets in the sty.

The girls bed the goats and gave some corn to the ducks and hens.

Ursula collected one hundred and twenty-seven eggs.

"What good workers you are!" said Mrs Ford. And she gave them all milk and biscuits in the farm kitchen.

"Now," said the farmer, "let me find you some more jobs."

"We haven't seen any lambs," said Ursula suddenly.

"The lambs aren't born yet," smiled the farmer. "The sheep are still out on the hillside. I'm sending Ben to fetch them home today, so the lambs can be born in the warm barn."

"Let me go with him," begged Ursula.

"It's a long way," warned the farmer. "But Ben will make sure you don't get lost. You'd better take your lunch with you."

Ursula put her bag over her shoulder and set off up the hill, with Ben leading the way.

Ben was a very clever dog. He

ran here and there, collecting the sheep together and turning them towards home.

But one sheep didn't want to come.

It stood on the edge of a rocky cliff, baaing loudly.

Ben ran behind the sheep to drive it away from the edge. But the sheep stamped its foot and would not move.

Ursula looked over the cliff.

"Oh, no!" she gasped.

A tiny lamb, only a few hours old, had fallen into a deep gully. It was lying on a ledge near the bottom, bleating in a weak small voice.

Ben dashed backwards and

forwards along the top of the gully and whined.

The sides were too steep, and there way no way he could get down to help the lamb.

Ursula knew she couldn't climb down either.

But she knew somebody who could.

In less than a minute, Ursula had unpacked the magic currant bun and was munching away so fast she almost choked.

"I'M A BEAR, I'M A BEAR, I'M A BEAR," she muttered. "I'M A BEAR, I'M A BEAR, I'M A BEAR."

Ben gave a sudden yelp and his

ears stood on end.

The girl in the blue dress had vanished.

And there, in her place, was a small brown bear.

With the lunch bag on her shoulder, Ursula Bear lowered herself over the edge of the gully.

Down and down she went, hanging on to rocks and brambles with her sharp claws.

And at last she reached the ledge where the little lamb was lying.

The lamb bleated in fright when it saw the bear.

"There, there," Ursula growled softly. "I won't hurt you."

And she gently lifted the baby

lamb into the bag.

Ben raced about barking when he saw Ursula scrambling back up the gully.

She reached the top at last, and soon the lamb was safely by its mother's side.

Ursula sat down for a rest, and to eat her beefburger.

"RAEB A M'I, RAEB A M'I RAEB A M'I," she growled, stuffing beefburger and chips into her mouth with her paws.

Ben wagged his tail hopefully, and his mouth watered as he watched every single mouthful.

Ursula saved him the very last bite.

And in no time at all Ursula was herself again, much to Ben's joy and relief.

he rounded up the sheep and set off down the hill towards the farm, his tail waving like a flag.

Ursula followed with the lamb in her arms.

Mr Ford was amazed when he saw the lamb.

"It's lucky you were there to bring it home," he said. "Come inside, Ursula. Everybody's having a nice big tea."

"Ben's earned one, too," said Ursula.

And she shared her scones and jam and cream with her new friend.

Alpha Beta and Grandma Delta

Meredith Hooper

Do you want to know what made big, handsome Alpha Beta, dog-with-a-bark-that-could-be-heard-in-the-next-street, angrier than anything?

Grandma Delta, old Grandma Delta cat, with twenty-three children and one hundred and twenty-one grandchildren, could leap up and over the garden fence, could leap any fence she met and *go wherever she liked*. Alpha Beta walked around the garden. Fence at the end, fence at each side, house and gate to the front, lawn in the middle with one tree. He knew it all. There was no way out for a dog. Same grass, same plants and same tree, every day.

Alpha Beta looked up at Grandma Delta lying relaxed along the branch of a tree. He growled. Grandma Delta flicked her tail. *How dare that cat sit in the tree?* thought Alpha Beta. There was no chance of reaching her. And she looked comfortable.

Grandma Delta was bored with
the tree. She sprang down, ran
along the path, leapt onto the top
of the fence, balanced – then with
one long leap she reached the
upstairs window sill at the side of
the house. The window sill was
warm in the sun. Grandma Delta
curled up and went to sleep.

Alpha Beta growled with rage. How dare that cat! He ran around the garden and back. Round the tree. *Bark! Bark!* He ran the other way round the tree. What was the use? Alpha Beta lay down, not looking at Grandma Delta, and pretended to sleep. Grandma Delta had not moved. High up on the window sill she could see about three gardens at once, if she wanted to.

Alpha Beta sighed. What was on the other side of the fence? He could not see through the fence, nor over it. He could only hear noises, and smell the smells. Alpha Beta dozed in the sun.

A sudden click woke him. Grandma Delta had padded past without him noticing and leapt up the fence. She paused, and was gone.

Alpha Beta put his nose in the air and howled with despair.

Something touched him on the paw. Alpha Beta looked through his howls and saw the most beautiful Fairy Dog.

"Oh, Alpha Beta," said the Fairy Dog. "I have come to grant you your wish."

"Let me do what that cat can do," breathed Alpha Beta.

"I will grant you your wish," said the Fairy Dog. "But you can only

100

un-wish it three times."

And she was gone.

Alpha Beta stood still. Thank goodness the Fairy Dog had not changed him into a cat! That would be terrible. But could he really do what a cat can do? Did he dare?

Alpha Beta looked up at the tree. He rushed at the trunk and threw his paws at it. A miracle! They held to the bark. He clambered up – up – to the branch where Grandma Delta always sat. It worked.

He felt dizzy with joy. Then he looked down. No, don't do that. Alpha Beta lay along the branch of the tree. The branch moved with the wind. Alpha Beta clung on tighter. The branch swayed, the light jigged between the leaves, and the ground looked a long way down. "I'm doing it, I'm doing it," chanted Alpha Beta to himself. "Just let Grandma Delta come back and she will see that I am here instead of her."

He held on a little tighter. "But I think that is probably enough for the first day and I'll get down now."

How? Suddenly Alpha Beta could not remember how Grandma Delta got down out of the tree. Front first? Not possible! Jump? It

was too far. He edged himself
along the branch towards the
trunk. Perhaps the back legs first?
But he didn't feel like letting go.
The branch seemed very narrow
and thin. "Oh, help!" cried Alpha
Beta. "I wish I was back on the
ground."

And he was.

That was much better. Good old
ground. It did not sway about.
"Just lack of practice," said Alpha
Beta to himself. "That is the only
problem, but I don't think I will go
back up into the tree at the
moment. I know," thought Alpha
Beta, "the window sill! That can't
move. It will be much better. I

should have tried it first."

As soon as he got up on the window sill Alpha Beta knew it was a mistake. The sill was far too narrow. It was terrible. "Help!" cried Alpha Beta, forgetting everything except how frightened he was. "Get me *down*."

And he was.

"Never, never, never again," said Alpha Beta.

But how silly he was being. The really important thing was the fence. Now he could get out. At long last he, Alpha Beta dog, could get over the fence and see what lay beyond.

Alpha Beta stood back. Then he ran a few steps forwards, leapt, clung briefly half-way up the fence – another leap up – balance on the top – and he was over.

The first thing Alpha Beta noticed was another fence. It looked like the one he had just come over. In fact everything looked rather the same. He was in another garden. There was a fence at the bottom, a fence at each side, grass, a tree. Alpha Beta was just going to inspect the bottom of the garden when there was a most awful noise.

"There's a dog! A dog in the garden! That dog from next door has got into our garden. Get him out!"

The shouts came louder, closer. Things were being thrown at him.

"Oh, get me out of here!" cried Alpha Beta. "I wish I was back home." And he was.

Alpha Beta dog lay on the grass. He supposed the Fairy Dog meant it when she said, "You can only

un-wish your wish three times".
But he did not mind. He did not
want to even try and see if he
could do what a cat can do.
Grandma Delta could dance on the
roof for all he cared. She could
swing upside down from the top of
the tree, or walk backwards along
every fence. He was staying where
he was.

But Grandma Delta had not seen
one of the awful things that had
happened. And that was all that
mattered.

The Winter Hedgehog

Ana and Reg Cartwright

One cold, misty autumn afternoon, the hedgehogs gathered in the wood. They were preparing for the long sleep of winter.

All, that is, except the smallest hedgehog. "What is winter?" he had asked his mother.

"Winter comes when we are asleep," she had replied. "It can be beautiful, but it can also be dangerous, cruel and very, very cold. It's not for the likes of us. Now go to sleep."

But the smallest hedgehog couldn't sleep. As evening fell he slipped away to look for winter. When hedgehogs are determined, they can move very swiftly, and soon the little hedgehog was far from home. An owl swooped down from high in a tree.

"Hurry home," he called. "It's time for your long sleep." But on and on went the smallest hedgehog until the sky turned dark and the trees were nothing but shadows.

The next morning, the hedgehog

awoke to find the countryside covered in fog. "Who goes there?" called a voice, and a large rabbit emerged from the mist.

"I'm looking for winter," replied the hedgehog. "Can you tell me where it is?"

"Hurry home," said the rabbit.

"Winter is on its way and it's no time for hedgehogs."

But the smallest hedgehog wouldn't listen. He was determined to find winter.

Days passed. The little hedgehog found plenty of slugs and insects to eat, but he couldn't find winter anywhere.

Then one day the air turned icy cold. Birds flew home to their roosts and the animals hid in their burrows and warrens. The smallest hedgehog felt very lonely and afraid and wished he was asleep with the other hedgehogs. But it was too late to turn back now.

That night winter came. A frosty

wind swept through the grass and blew the last straggling leaves from the trees. In the morning the whole countryside was covered in a carpet of snow.

"Winter!" cried the smallest hedgehog. "I've found it at last." And all the birds flew down from the trees to join him.

The trees were completely bare and the snow sparkled on the grass. The little hedgehog went to the river to drink, but it was frozen. He shivered, shook his prickles and stepped onto the ice. His feet began to slide and the faster he scurried, the faster he sped across it. "Winter is

wonderful," he cried. At first he did not see the fox, like a dark shadow slinking towards him.

"Hello! Come and join me," he called as the fox reached the river bank. But the fox only heard the rumble of his empty belly. With one leap he pounced onto the ice. When the little hedgehog saw his sly yellow eyes he understood what the fox was about. He curled into a ball and spiked his prickles.

"Ouch!" cried the fox. The sharp prickles stabbed his paws and he reeled towards the centre of the river where he disappeared beneath the ice.

"That was close," the smallest

hedgehog cried to himself. "Winter is beautiful, but it is also cruel, dangerous and very, very cold."

Colder and colder it grew until the snow froze under the hedgehog's feet. The snow came again and a cruel north wind picked it up and whipped it into a blizzard. "Winter is dangerous and cruel and very, very cold," moaned the little hedgehog.

Luck saved him. A hare scurrying home gave him shelter in his burrow. By morning the snow was still falling, but gently now, covering everything in a soft white blanket.

The smallest hedgehog was enchanted as he watched the pattern his paws made. Reaching the top of a hill, he rolled into a ball and spun over and over, turning himself into a great white snowball as he went. Down and down he rolled until he reached the feet of two children building a snowman.

"Hey, look at this," said the little girl. "A perfect head for our snowman."

"I'm a hedgehog," he cried. But no one heard his tiny hedgehog voice.

The girl placed the hedgehog snowball on the snowman's body

116

and the boy used a carrot for a nose and pebbles for the eyes.

When the children had gone, the cold and hungry hedgehog nibbled at the carrot nose. As he munched the sun came out and the snow began to melt. He blinked in the bright sunlight, tumbled down the snowman's body and was free.

Time went on. The hedgehog saw the world in its winter cloak. He saw red berries disappear from the hedgerows as the birds collected them for their winter larders. And he watched children speed down the hill on their sleighs.

The winter passed. One day the air grew warmer and the river

117

began to flow again. The little hedgehog found crocuses and snowdrops beneath the trees and he knew it was time to go home. Slowly he made his way back to the wood.

From out of every log, sleepy hedgehogs were emerging from their long sleep.

"Where have you been?" they called to him.

"I found winter," he replied.

"And what was it like?" asked his mother.

"It was beautiful, but it was also . . ."

"Dangerous, cruel and very, very cold," finished his mother.

But she was answered by a yawn, a sigh and a snore, and the smallest hedgehog was fast asleep.

Eight Hairy Legs

David Henry Wilson

There was a spider in the bath. Jeremy James was sitting on the lavatory, and he just happened to look sideways and downwards, and there was the spider. It wasn't one of those tiny, tickly ones – he didn't mind those. No, it was one of those large leg-spreading ones, black and hairy and shuddery – the sort that make your backbone run up and down your body.

It's not easy to think about other things when there's a black spider sprawling less than three feet away from your bare legs. At any moment it could come scrabbling up the bath and onto your foot, legs, tummy . . . ugh! Besides, where there's one spider there could be other spiders, and there's just no telling where they might crawl to.

Jeremy James immediately felt a goose-pimply tingle at the back of his neck, and slapped it hard to make sure the goose pimple didn't creep down onto his back. Then the thought occurred to him that if a spider got into the bath, another spider might get into the lavatory, and then just think where that could creep to! He leapt off the seat and looked into the pan. Nothing.

He looked down into the bath again, just in time to see the spider take a quick scuttly step towards the plughole. Then it stopped still again, legs slightly bent, as if tensed to do a mighty leap. If it leapt out of the bath, Jeremy James decided he would leap out of the bathroom. But what should he do if it stayed in the bath?

Jeremy James remembered a spider that had once been hanging on his bedroom wall. He had known then that he'd never be able to sleep while it was there, and so he'd taken his bedroom slipper and given the spider a whack. But the result had been a horrible mess. Half the spider had been squelched into the wall, and the other half had been squelched into the slipper, and Mummy had had to come and wipe all the bits and pieces away with a wet cloth. Even then, Jeremy James hadn't slept very well, because he kept imagining spider-legs running all over him.

On another occasion he'd called for Daddy, and Daddy had arrived with a large sheet of newspaper.

"Let's have a look then," Daddy had said, and with the newspaper spread wide he had advanced on the spider and had suddenly jammed the paper against the wall and at great speed screwed it up into a big ball.

"He won't trouble you any more," Daddy had said. "He's either dead or studying the sports news."

But Jeremy James had seen something Daddy had not seen, and he asked Daddy to unscrew the paper again. And when Daddy unscrewed the paper, he found to his surprise that there was nothing there except the sports news. Then they had spent half an hour trying in vain to attract a spider that clearly wasn't interested in sport. That had been another sleepless night.

Well, at least this was morning, and the spider was in the bathroom, not the bedroom. But the problem was the same – how do you get rid of a spider without making it into a mess or a magic vanishing act?

The spider twitched and twiddled itself one step nearer the plughole. Jeremy James had an idea. Another few steps and it would be near enough for him to turn the tap on and swoosh it away down the hole. No mess at all. In fact, as clean an end as you could wish for.

"Move!" said Jeremy James. "Go on! Shoo! Quick march!"

The spider did not even slow-march. Jeremy James stood and looked at the spider, and the spider stood and looked at Jeremy James. This was not going to be easy. Jeremy James needed a weapon, and his eye fell on the bathbrush. A scratch with those bristles should make even the toughest spider jump. It might even take the brush for a monster with a moustache and die of fright.

Jeremy James ran the bathbrush

along the bottom of the bath, until the bristles were almost touching what might be the spider's eighth little toenail. The spider remained very still. Jeremy James moved the brush again so that it just touched the tip of the spidery toe. The spider twitched. Probably thought

it had an itch. Jeremy James pushed the brush firmly against the spider's leg. With a scurry and a flurry the spider raced forward, while Jeremy James leapt back and dropped the brush in the bath with a clatter.

Now his heart was jumping like a grasshopper with hiccups. This was turning out to be a dangerous battle. In the past he'd killed snakes and crocodiles and man-eating tigers in the bath, but none of them had given him half as much trouble as this spider. There it lurked, hairy legs spread wide apart, waiting to pounce and cover him with shivers. Two inches away

128

from the plughole.

Gradually Jeremy James's heart sat down again in his chest. If he could just push the spider with the brush and then whoosh it with the tap, he could send it sailing down the Seven Seas. On the other hand, it might grab hold of the brush and come racing over the bristles, handle, hand, arm . . .

Heroes don't think about "might-be"s. Jeremy James leaned over the bath, picked up the brush, and with eyes swivelling like tennis-watchers he reached for the tap nearest the spider.

Swoosh and sweep! Down came the water and the brush, and as

the spider struggled to swim up
the bath, so Jeremy James pushed
it down again. But the flow of
water kept bringing the spider
back up the bath. Jeremy James
turned the tap off, and the water
sucked the spider back towards
the hole.

"Down you go!" said Jeremy
James.

And with eight despairing waves
and a loud gurgle, the spider
disappeared from view.

Bathbrush in hand, Jeremy
James stood triumphant.

"Jeremy James!" came Mummy's
voice from the landing. "Haven't
you finished in there?"

"I've just been killing a spider," said Jeremy James.

"Well hurry up. I'm waiting to bath the twins!" called Mummy.

"It was a huge spider!" said Jeremy James. "And it nearly killed *me*!"

But Mummy didn't seem interested. Perhaps she might have been more interested if the spider *had* killed Jeremy James. Then she might have wished she'd thought more about spiders and less about baths and twins.

Jeremy James sat down on the lavatory again, legs dangling and lips pouting. What was the use of being a hero if nobody was interested? He glanced sadly down at the scene of his heroism – and his glance got stuck into a long and disbelieving stare: there, on the edge of the plughole, looking a little damp and dazed and drippy, was the ghost of the drowned spider.

Jeremy James leapt off the lavatory as if it had been a pincushion. "Mummy!" he cried.

"What is it?" asked Mummy from one of the bedrooms.

"There's a spider in the bath!" cried Jeremy James.

"I thought you'd killed it," said Mummy, now on the landing.

Jeremy James unlocked the

bathroom door, and Mummy came in.

"Ugh!" she said. "What a monster!"

"I did kill it," said Jeremy James, "but it must have unkilled itself."

"Well, this is what we do with spiders," said Mummy. On the bathroom shelf, next to the toothbrush stand, was the mouthwash glass, which Mummy picked up in her right hand. With her left, she tore off a sheet of toilet paper. "Now watch carefully," she said.

Then she bent over the bath, and put the glass upside down round the spider. She slid the sheet of paper under the glass and under the spider, turned the glass the right way up, and plop! There was the spider sitting at the bottom of the glass.

"He doesn't look quite so big now, does he?" said Mummy, holding the glass so that Jeremy James could see.

In fact the spider seemed quite small and silly, sitting there looking out at Jeremy James looking in.

"What shall we do with him?" asked Mummy.

"Can we throw him out of the window?" suggested Jeremy James.

"Good idea," said Mummy.

She opened the window, leaned out, and with a flick of her wrist sent the spider diving down to the lawn below. Then she showed Jeremy James the empty glass, which she washed out and replaced on the bathroom shelf.

"Can spiders fly?" asked Jeremy James.

"Yes," said Mummy. "But only downwards."

Mummy left the bathroom, and Jeremy James perched on the lavatory again. It was amazing how simple things were when Mummy did them. He looked all round the bathroom, hoping to see another spider so that he could do the trick with the glass and paper. But there wasn't a spider to be seen.

There was just one thing about Mummy's trick that slightly worried Jeremy James. It was nothing very important, but when a little later he cleaned his teeth, he rinsed his mouth with water straight from the tap. He didn't really need a glass for that anyway.

How the Animals Got Tails

Anne English

There once was a time when none of the animals in the world had tails – not a single one. The horse had no tail to swish away the flies. The dog had no tail to wag when he was happy. And the monkey had no tail to curl round the branches when he was jumping from tree to tree.

The wise lion, who was king of the animals, knew there was something missing, and he thought and thought until he had a clever idea.

"Animals. Animals," he roared, "I, the lion, the king of all the animals, command you to come to a meeting in the Great Meadow. Roar, roar!"

When they heard the lion roar every animal from far and near came hurrying to the Great Meadow. First came the fox and the squirrel, then the horse, the dog and the cat. Then came the monkey and the mouse. The lion waited for them all to arrive. "Sit in a circle round me," he told them, "and hear what I have to say." More and more animals came until the circle was almost complete. The elephant and the pig were nearly late, but last of all was the rabbit. He had been eating a carrot when he heard the lion roar, and had finished it before coming to the Great Meadow. And now he was the very last to arrive.

The lion held up his paw for silence. "Friends," he said, "I have been thinking." He paused. "I have been thinking that something is missing for all of us, so I have invented – TAILS." And he help up a huge bag full of tails.

"You will get one each," he told the animals, "and wear your own always." How the animals clapped and cheered their clever leader. "Now, first come, first served," said the lion, "and as I was here first I get the first tail." And from the bag he pulled a marvellous long golden tail with a black tassel at the end, and put it on himself. How wonderful it made him look. He waved it proudly, while the animals watched, and waited for their tails.

The lion stood in the circle and called out, "The fox."

He gave the fox a long, thick bushy tail, like a brush. Fox put it

140

on and went away proudly.

"Next, the squirrel," said the
lion. And the squirrel too got a
huge bushy tail, which he curved
up over his back before leaping
away.

The horse came next, and from
the bag the lion pulled a long,

strong, black tail, combed out until it was silky and straight. The horse was delighted, and galloped off swishing his new tail from side to side.

The cat and the dog came into the circle together, and they each received a straight tail, which would wave or wag from side to

side, or up and down, as they pleased.

The monkey was given an extremely long tail. He curled it over his arm, so that he wouldn't trip over it, and went jumping away into the trees.

By now the bag of tails was half empty, so there was not much choice for the elephant when he came in his turn. In fact his tail looked like a piece of chewed string – just look at it, if you see an elephant. But he put it on quite happily, and lumbered off.

"Mouse," called the lion, and the mouse came. Now considering how small a mouse is, he did very well, for the tail pulled from the bag for him was very long indeed. Mouse put it on and scuttled away, trailing his tail behind him.

"Humph!" said the lion, as the pig came up. "Not much left now," and he took out yet another straight stringy tail. The pig was not pleased. "The elephant and the mouse have tails like that," he said. "Can I have something different, please?" The lion shook his head.

"Sorry," he said, "you arrived almost last, and this is all there is."

"Oh, very well then," said the pig, taking the stringy tail and

144

looking at it crossly.

"This will just not suit me," he muttered. "Just imagine a pig with a straight tail!" As he walked away he trod on a thick twig. "Hoink, hoink," he grunted, "I have an idea. Lions aren't the only ones with brains."

And he took his tail and wrapped it tightly round the twig. When he pulled the twig out the tail stayed curly. "I like that better," pig said, and he stuck on his new curly tail.

Last of all to receive a tail was the rabbit. By now the lion was rather tired of tails, and he hurriedly shook the bag upside down to get out the last one. It was

tiny – just a tiny thin piece of tail.
Poor rabbit was disappointed, but
he knew there was nothing else, so
he thanked the lion and took the
tail. But it was so small he
couldn't bring himself to put it on.

"This is just a nothing tail," he
told himself. "Not a bushy tail like
the fox's, or swishy like the
horse's. Not even long enough to
wave or wag. I will look silly with
this one." He sighed. The lion had
given them all tails, and they
would have to wear them, rabbit
knew.

As the rabbit wandered along,
thinking about his piece of tail, he
came to a prickly bush, and *he* had

a wonderful idea. "Rabbits can think as well as lions and pigs," he said. And he took his tail and stroked it gently backwards and forwards over the prickles, until the tail became soft and round. *That's better*, thought rabbit, looking at it happily. Then he stuck on his new fluffy tail, and bobbed away merrily.

The Tale of Brave Augustus

Annette Elizabeth Clark

Once upon a time an old woman whose name was Mrs Popple lived in a little white cottage among wide green fields. The cottage had a garden where Mrs Popple grew potatoes and onions and cabbages and carrots, and there was a border of flowers each side of the path that led to the garden gate. Beyond the gate there was a little pond with reeds and rushes by its edge; and on the pond lived Augustus, Mrs Popple's large white gander. Once there had been two geese upon the pond, for Augustus had a wife who was named Augusta. But Augusta had died, and since then Augustus had been all alone.

Mrs Popple was very kind to him. She fed him well (in fact, she fed him so well that Augustus was far too fat to fly). When she called to him, Augustus would come waddling to meet her, with his long neck stretched out, all ready to take nice bits of fat and soaked bread and juicy cabbage. She often chatted to him, and sometimes when she walked in the fields on spring evenings to look for early primroses or violets in the hedges, Augustus would go with her. He gabbled while Mrs Popple talked, and while Mrs Popple picked flowers Augustus picked slugs and snails and fresh green blades of young grass; so they both enjoyed their walk.

But in spite of all this, Augustus was sometimes very lonely. He longed for a real companion.

Mrs Popple had two cats; their names were Daisy and Dora. She had two rabbits; their names were

James and John. She had quite a
family of chickens and two hives of
bees. All her pets had companions
except poor Augustus; and though
she and Augustus talked to each
other in their own way, Augustus
often felt he could say much more
if he had another goose to speak
to.

One fine evening in April Mrs
Popple came down her garden
path. Spring really had come at
last. Her clumps of double
daffodils had pointed green buds
and big yellow flowers. Her red
and yellow polyanthuses were all
in bloom. There were white violets
and blue violets tucked in among

the stones by the gate, and the fat green shoots on her lilac tree were all unfolding. The grass smelled fresh and the wind was soft. "It's a pleasant evening," said Mrs Popple. "I shall take a little walk."

She called to Augustus and he came sailing to the edge of the pond. The bank was very low on the side nearest the cottage, and Augustus stepped out and waddled after Mrs Popple. Daisy and Dora, the cats, came a little way with them, and then Mrs Popple was stooping down to pick primroses in a little lane when she noticed that Augustus was behaving very oddly. He was trying to stand on tiptoe (and you know that his feet were not really the right shape for that). He was flapping his wings and stretching his long neck and calling "Ga-ga-ga" very loudly.

"Whatever is the matter, Augustus dear?" said Mrs Popple.

She looked up at the sky as Augustus was looking, and high overhead she saw three great birds come flying – three big grey birds, with wide wings and long stretched-out necks.

"Oh!" said Mrs Popple. "It's the wild geese. There they go, flying north with the spring, to make their nests. Don't you try to go with them and leave me, Augustus dear."

Augustus said, "Ga-ga-ga" and flapped his wings again. The wild geese took no notice of his calling. They flew on fast and steadily. But some way behind them came another goose. It was flying slowly. It seemed very tired, and it was getting slower ever minute and flying lower and lower still.

"Augustus," said Mrs Popple, "that goose must have hurt its wing. It won't fly far. I shouldn't be surprised if it came down in the Marsh. I hope the fox won't get it, poor thing."

But of course all Augustus could say to her was "Ga-ga-ga" again. It was really very awkward for him

to have no one really to talk to when he had so much to say. For Augustus was full of excitement to think that another goose was so near. *Perhaps if I could find her, she would stay on the pond with me*, he thought. And he made up his mind to go and look for the goose that very night.

Late that evening, Mrs Popple stood at her garden gate calling for Augustus. She called and called, but no Augustus came waddling across the field. At last Mrs Popple shut the door of the shed where Augustus always slept with James and John and she went indoors. She went to bed very worried. She was certain that something had happened to her dear Augustus. She scarcely slept all night, and before the sun was up next morning she stood by her garden gate calling and calling again.

You and I know what had happened of course, but Mrs Popple did not. Augustus had gone. He had gone to look for the goose that was hurt. He did not know where the Marsh was, but he was determined to find out. (Perhaps I had better explain, in case you do not know, that a Marsh is a place where the ground is soft and wet, with reeds and

157

rushes and water-plants growing on it.)

When he came back with Mrs Popple from their walk together, he swam round and round the pond, thinking about it all. When Mrs Popple went indoors to get her supper, Augustus came out of the pond and hurried away, across the field. He could go quite fast for a short distance because he flapped his wings and that helped him to run. But he soon got out of breath and had to go more slowly.

It was growing dark by that time and Augustus had never been out alone after dusk. But the sky looked very high and wide and clear; two or three bright stars were twinkling and there was a silver-shining half-moon. "Plenty of light to see by," said Augustus bravely to himself, and he waddled on with his little black shadow beside him in the moonlight.

He was just squeezing through a gap in a hedge when suddenly a big brown hare jumped up right in front of him out of a ditch. It frightened Augustus terribly, and he had just opened his beak to say "Ga-ga-ga" very loudly when he remembered that he had better not make a noise, or Mrs Popple might find him and drive him home. So he only said, in a rather panting voice, "Please could you tell me the way to the Marsh? I want to find the goose that has hurt her wing."

"Certainly I can tell you; I saw the goose myself," said the hare. "Shall I come with you? I might be some use."

"Yes, do come," said Augustus. So they went on together with their two little black shadows in the moonlight, and Augustus felt very glad to have the hare for company.

They were going very quietly and carefully across the grass when a very loud "Buzz-zz-zz" just beside his yellow foot, made poor

160

Augustus jump again. It was a
bumble-bee that had stayed out too
late. He was sitting on a
dandelion, cold and cross and
sleepy, and he was afraid that
Augustus might gobble him up
with his yellow bill. But when
Augustus and the hare explained
where they were going, the
bumble-bee said, "I saw the goose
too. Shall I come with you? I might
be some use."

"Yes, do come," said Augustus.
He could not quite see what use
the bumble-bee could be; but he
said to himself, "Every little
helps." So he let the bumble-bee
crawl up his yellow bill and onto

his feathery white head. It was tickly for Augustus, but the feathers were warm and comfortable for the bumble-bee. So they went on together with their three little black shadows in the moonlight. The bumble-bee's shadow made a little bump on the top of Augustus's head.

Presently they came to a high green bank with a gate in it. The gate stood open, and they were just going to pass through when something small and fluffy and noisy bounced out of a hole in the bank and hit poor Augustus in one eye. "Chit-chit-chit-cheep-cheep-chitter-chee," it said in a very shrill voice. Augustus thought that some fierce creature was trying to bite his head off. But it was only a little brown jenny-wren that had waked up suddenly in a fright when she heard them coming. And when they explained where they were going, Jenny-wren said, "I saw the goose, too. Shall I come with you?"

"Yes, do come," said Augustus. Jenny-wren perched herself on his tail feathers, and they went on together with their four little black shadows in the moonlight. Jenny-wren's shadow made a lump on the end of Augustus's tail.

By this time they were going

163

downhill to the Marsh. They were passing some bushes when there was a very loud sneeze, so loud that Augustus jumped with fright and almost ran away. But it was only a little old brown donkey who was standing half asleep in the shadow. They told him where they were going and he said, "I know where the goose is. She is hiding in the Marsh. Shall I come with you?"

"Yes, do come," said Augustus, and they went on together with their five black shadows in the moonlight. The donkey went first, and the hare and Augustus with the bumble-bee and Jenny-wren followed close behind him.

They were close to the edge of
the Marsh when suddenly the
donkey stopped. He put his head
down; his long brown ears stood
straight up and then they pointed
forward. Augustus and the hare
peeped out from behind the
donkey's tail. They crept forward
to see what he was looking at. He

was standing at the edge of a wide ditch, staring at a big fox that was creeping along in the shadow. They had come so softly over the grass that the fox had not heard them. His ears were pricked, his eyes were shining, his bushy tail trailed behind him. Quickly and quietly he was crawling down to the Marsh to catch the goose that had hurt her wing.

And all at once Augustus quite forgot about being frightened. "Ga-ga-ga," he cried and flapped his wings. It surprised the hare so much that he jumped straight into the ditch, right on top of the fox. Augustus jumped too. He caught the fox's tail with his strong beak and pinched and tweaked with all his might. The fox snarled and turned to snap at Augustus. "Buzz-zz-zz," said the bumble-bee and bumped the fox on his nose, while Jenny-wren shrieked, "Chee-chee-chee-chee-e-e-p" and flew straight into his eyes, and the donkey brayed and brayed with all his might.

The fox could not think what had happened to him. He had never been so frightened in all his life. He gave a wriggle and a jump and the next minute he was out of the ditch and running across the field. He ran and ran, and never stopped running till he was safe in his den in the wood; and he stayed there the rest of the night.

But Augustus did not stop to see what the fox was doing. He could hear a flapping and a fluttering and an anxious goose-voice calling. He spread his wings wide and ran. The goose with the lame wing was calling from the Marsh where she had been trying to hide among some clumps of big yellow marsh marigolds and tall dead reeds and bulrushes. Her wing was too stiff to fly, and the fox would have caught her quite easily.

Augustus ran to her and stroked her with his bill. He talked to her in goose-language, and told her she was safe and that he would take care of her and take her to his home. The grey goose talked to him and told him all her troubles and how a man had shot at her and hurt her wing. By and by they had a little sleep; the bumble-bee buzzed to itself in a yellow marsh marigold, and Jenny-wren chirped sleepily in a willow tree, and the donkey and the hare nibbled grass.

So they all spent the rest of the night together, feeling happy and proud and contented, and in the morning Augustus thanked his kind friends and they all set out across the fields to their homes.

Mrs Popple was standing at her garden gate. She had been there since daybreak, as you know, calling for Augustus. She was beginning to feel most sadly sure that she would never see him again. She watched the sun rise out of a grey mist, she saw the dewdrops sparkle and twinkle all over the green grass. It was a pretty morning, but she could not feel happy when Augustus was lost. "Au-gus-tus, Augustus!" she called again and again. And then all of a sudden she stopped. "I do believe I hear his voice!" said Mrs Popple.

She listened and she heard it

quite plainly. Augustus was talking to the grey goose; and then she saw them both. They squeezed through the hole in the hedge and came stepping proudly and happily across the field in the sunshine.

"Bless me," said Mrs Popple, "my brave Augustus! He's found the goose that was hurt and brought it home."

She ran into the house and came out with a pan full of lovely scraps and soaked bread and mutton fat, greens and a large crumbled bit of cake (which she put in extra because she was so happy). She put the pan down and Augustus and the grey goose scurried to it, and emptied it in a great hurry. They were both very hungry. Then they waddled to the pond, and soon they were washing themselves and tidying their feathers as if they had both lived there all their lives.

The grey goose's wing never quite got well again. It was always too stiff to fly far. But she did not seem to mind. She settled down on Mrs Popple's pond, and she and Augustus brought up family after family of fluffy yellow goslings. Augustus never felt lonely again, and he and the grey goose loved each other dearly as long as they lived. So I think you might say that the end of this story is, "They lived happily ever after."

Pussy Simkin Meets a Peacock Bird

Linda Greenbury

Pussy Simkin was sitting in the sun. He had just finished washing his fine, fat tail when he saw his friend, Siamese Ching, walking along the high fence.

"Good afternoon, Pussy Simkin," said Ching.

"Good afternoon, Siamese Ching. What shall we do today?"

"I'll take you to the park today, but first you have got to get out of this garden." Siamese Ching dropped gently down onto the flower bed. "Come here, Pussy Simkin," he said, "and let's see you jump."

Pussy Simkin stood up, and shook his tail. It looked handsome, he thought, with the white bits all white, and the orange parts bright and silky. He walked over to Siamese Ching and, taking a deep breath, he leant on his back legs, looked at the high, high fence, and jumped.

"Mi-Ho! Mi-Ho! Mi-Ho!" cried Siamese Ching, as Pussy Simkin

"plonked" back onto the flower bed. "That's no good, try again!"

Pussy Simkin tried again, with a deeper breath, and a bigger lean backwards. And he fell back onto the flower bed with a bigger plonk. Siamese Ching said, "Higher, higher, Pussy Simkin, try again!"

Once, twice, three times, Pussy Simkin tried to jump onto the fence, but each time he fell into the flowers.

Siamese Ching showed his fat, furry friend how to do it, but he still plonked back. The two cats wondered what to do. It was no good thinking of going to the park if Pussy Simkin couldn't even get out of the garden!

Siamese Ching had an idea. "Let's walk carefully round the garden. Maybe somewhere there's a gap and you can squeeze through."

Sure enough, halfway down one side, there was a gap, and Pussy Simkin began to squeeze through his head, then his neck, then his front paws and then his body. But, then, he got stuck. Siamese Ching roared and roared with laughter.

"Oh dear! Oh dear! You do look funny!" he said.

Pussy Simkin didn't think it was at all funny. "Don't just stand there laughing," he said. "Push me

– or pull me – *do* something."

Siamese Ching gave a hard push at his friend's back. Pussy Simkin turned and twisted – twisted and turned – and suddenly he was through the gap. Siamese Ching jumped up onto the top of the fence and down on the other side. Pussy Simkin looked at his tail. It wasn't so beautiful now, all muddy from the flower bed, and all tangled from the fence.

"You can't stop and wash it now," said Siamese Ching. "Come on – we're going to cross the road."

Pussy Simkin walked with Siamese Ching to the edge of the road. Siamese Ching showed his friend how to watch the cars rush by, and how to look to the left and look to the right and look again to the left and make sure the road was empty before trying to cross. They they marched quickly together to the other side, and went into the park.

"Carefully now," whispered Siamese Ching. "Don't let the park-keeper see you; he doesn't like cats in his park."

Pussy Simkin followed Siamese Ching along a muddy path. They crept past a house where, Siamese Ching said, the park-keeper lived, and ran softly, without a sound up a grassy slope.

They stopped, and Siamese Ching said, "Well, Pussy Simkin, how's that for a place to play?"

As far as Pussy Simkin could see, stretched beautiful green grass. It was bigger than the farmyard he had lived in before. It was smoother and greener than the fields where he used to watch the birds in the country. It was surely the biggest, finest garden Pussy Simkin had ever seen.

"Wow. Mia-ow-wow-wow!" he said. "This is verrry nice!"

The two cats walked all the way round this big, grassy garden, looking under a little gate to see some flowers, and over a low wall to watch the sparrows. Siamese Ching made sure the park-keeper was looking the other way, and they peeped at the fish pond, and saw the golden fish swimming round and round under a fountain.

Suddenly, Pussy Simkin heard a terrible noise: *Caw! Caaaaw!*

Caaaaaw! He arched his back and looked very frightened.

"Whatever's that?" he said.

"That's a peacock."

"A peacock?"

"A bird, with a long tail of many colours."

"I don't like it," Pussy Simkin said. "I shall go and chase it away."

And he began to run towards the tree where the noise came from.

"Pussy Simkin, come back!" called Siamese Ching. "The peacock belongs to the park! Leave it alone! Come back!"

"I'm going to chase it away," called Pussy Simkin, looking very determined. "Don't fuss so, I'm very good at chasing birds."

Pussy Simkin reached the tree. He could see a dark shape up in the branches. "Caw! Caaaaw! Caaaaaaaw!" it said.

"*Pssssssssssst!*" said Pussy Simkin in his fiercest voice. "*Pssssssssssst!* Go away, silly little bird, *pssssssssssst!*"

There was a flutter of wings, and a rush of wind, and out of the branches and down to the ground flew the bird. It was enormous! It was bigger than a pigeon – bigger than Pussy Simkin himself, and its long tail stretched behind it like a carpet, on the ground.

Pussy Simkin didn't remember

seeing a bird this big before. His
fierce voice was suddenly lost, and
his proud arched back lay flat.

He began to walk slowly
backwards, and the peacock bird
began to walk forwards saying,
"Caw! Caaaaw! Caaaaaaaw! Go
away, silly orange cat, you go away!
This is my park. Caw! Caw! Caw!"
And the peacock bird did a funny
little twist, and a flutter – rush –
whoosh of his feathers, and there
was his beautiful many-coloured
tail all spread out and standing up
behind him.

Pussy Simkin ran as fast as he
could. He didn't wait for Siamese
Ching, he didn't look for the

park-keeper. He ran home past the grassy slope, past the park-keeper's house, along the muddy path, across the road. He was in such a hurry that he forgot about the big high fence around his own little garden, and he jumped right over it, in one try!

Pussy Simkin looked at his tail.

Poor tail! All muddy and dirty and tangled! he began to lick it clean again.

And Siamese Ching? Well, he was sitting in the tree where the peacock bird had been, watching it walk proudly across the big, grassy park. And Siamese Ching was thinking of Pussy Simkin and smiling his Siamese smile.

The Rat Wedding

Andrew Matthews

At the end of Hall Avenue stood a ruined mansion where the squire of Boggart Hollow once lived. When Mr and Mrs Rat moved into the mansion with their daughter Rita, Mrs Rat was delighted. "We can't mix with riff-raff now we live here," she told her husband. "It wouldn't suit the neighbourhood." And she set about teaching Rita good manners.

"Whenever you gnaw a piece of mouldy cheese, Rita, be sure to hold out your little claws," said Mrs Rat. "And never let your tail dangle over the edge of a dustbin when you're inside; it's not polite."

Rita soon grew tired of her mother's fussy ways, but she did as she was told and never once complained.

So it came as a great shock when one day Rita walked into me dining room arm in arm with a young male rat. "This is Ricky, Mother!" she said. "We want to get married!"

"Married?" cried Mrs Rat, twiddling her whiskers. She lifted her head and looked haughtily

188

down her nose at Ricky. "Have you come here to ask for my daughter's paw in marriage?" she demanded.

"Yuss, that's the up and down of it," said Ricky. "Me and Rita want to get hitched, like."

"I'm afraid that's quite impossible!" said Mrs Rat. "My

daughter moves in the highest society, and you wouldn't make a suitable husband at all!"

"But he's lovely!" Rita wailed. "He can squeak and scamper like anything, and this tail is as slithery as a snake."

"There's more to marriage than a slithery tail," said Mrs Rat.

And that was that. No matter how Rita wept, or how Mr Rat pleaded with her to change her mind, Mrs Rat stayed firm. "I won't have my daughter marrying someone common!" she declared. "As a matter of fact, I have someone in mind – one of the highest people in the land."

"Who's that?" asked Mr Rat.

"The sun," Mrs Rat replied. "It's noon, so he should be right overhead. Let's go into the garden and speak to him."

The sun was high in the sky, shining down on the trees and flowers. He noticed the rats staring up at him, and he smiled at them in a polite sort of way. "Good afternoon," he said.

"Mr Sun," said Mrs Rat. "I'll come straight to the point. You're famous the world over, and your strength is second to none. I'm pleased to tell you that I've decided you should be Rita's husband!"

"Me, strong?" said the sun. "See that cloud over there? When he floats across my face, everything goes dark. He's far stronger than I am. He's the one you're looking for."

The cloud was alarmed when he heard this. He loved being free, and sailing across the sky, and he didn't want to marry anyone – especially a rat. "I'm not strong at all!" he said quickly. "I'm a real wimp compared to the wind. As soon as he blows, I go flying all over the place. The wind is the one you should be talking to."

The wind happened to be in the garden at that very moment. He was rattling the leaves on the trees and making the flowers nod their heads.

"Mr Wind," said Mrs Rat. "Mr Cloud, who is far stronger than Mr Sun, tells me that you are stronger than he is, so you must marry my daughter!"

"Strong?" said the wind. "I'm useless compared to your old garden wall. If you stand behind him when I'm blowing my hardest, you won't feel a thing."

At this, Rita burst into tears and stamped her paws on the ground. "I don't care what you say, Mother," she sobbed, "I'm *not* getting married to the garden wall!"

"You won't have to, don't you worry," said the wall. "I might look pretty solid and reliable, but take a look at that big hole in my middle. That was made by someone far stronger than I am."

"Who?" said Mrs Rat.

"Why, Ricky Rat, of course!" chuckled the wall. "He dug his way right through me so he could meet Rita secretly in the garden. A rat is the strongest thing in the world – everybody knows that!"

And so Rita and Ricky were married, and Mrs Rat invited all her posh friends to the wedding feast.

"My dear," one of them said to

her, "wherever did you find Rita such a fine young husband?"

"Some very important friends of ours told us about him," said Mrs Rat. "We were thinking of marrying Rita to the sun, but of course, Ricky is *so* much stronger!"

Mr Buffin and Harold Trotter

Robert Hartman

Harold Trotter was the name of Mr Buffin's pig. He was called Harold after Mr Buffin's uncle, General Sir Harold Buffin KCB, and Trotter because that happened to be his name. Mr Buffin's uncle, a very famous man, had been governor of several places where it was always very hot and very wet, and Mr Buffin hoped that Harold Trotter would live up to the name of Harold and become a very famous pig.

But Harold Trotter showed very little promise of becoming famous. He was in fact a simple-minded pig, and it meant nothing to him what Mr Buffin's uncle had done or where he had been. Harold Trotter had but three interests in life, and they were eating, sleeping and having his back scratched. These, he thought, were the chief things in life and the only things worth thinking about.

Sometimes when Mr Buffin was walking in the neighbourhood of

Harold Trotter's sty, he would take a bamboo cane from the potting shed in the garden and scratch Harold Trotter's back with it. Harold Trotter would remain quite still enjoying the lovely shivers that ran up and down his spine. Every now and then he would express his pleasure in little grunts and squeaks of delight, and when Mr Buffin stopped scratching he would give a louder squeak, which was his way of asking for more.

The sty was Harold Trotter's home, but as the door was always left open he was free to wander where he pleased. Mr Buffin left the door open on purpose because he thought that life in a pigsty must be a very boring sort of life, and that if Harold Trotter was free to wander where he pleased it might help him to become a famous pig. When Harold Trotter was outside the sty he would wander around the garden scratching his back against all sorts of things. Some things made better scratching things than others, and Harold Trotter had several favourite scratching places.

One favourite scratching place was the row of young trees that Mr Buffin had planted beside the drive that led up to the house. The stems of the trees were springy, and that made them really good scratchers. Other favourite places were a garden seat, a drainpipe and a water-butt into which ran the rainwater from the roof.

It was this habit of looking for scratching places that got Harold Trotter into very serious trouble, such serious trouble that it was nearly the end of him. Even now, when the trouble is all over, Harold Trotter hates to think about how serious it was.

It happened like this. One day when Mr Buffin was walking round his garden, thinking of nothing in particular but having a good look at everything, he noticed that a white climbing rose, called White Knite, which grew up the side of his house, wanted tying back to the wall.

"Dear me," said Mr Buffin, when he saw the roses swaying to and fro on the end of their branches, "that means getting a ladder."

Mr Buffin did not like ladders; that is to say he had nothing against ladders in themselves, but he disliked fetching them, carrying them and climbing up them. All of which sounds as though he had a great many ladders; actually he had only one.

And yet another reason for disliking them: he always felt giddy when he got to the top of a ladder. Like many other people, Mr Buffin could not look down from a height. It made him think about what it would be like to fall through the air and to go on falling until the bottom was reached. And that made him feel giddy.

However, Mr Buffin tried to forget all about giddiness and heights, and went round to the potting shed, took the ladder off the hooks on which it hung and carried it round to the front of the house. He then placed the ladder against the wall behind the climbing rose.

"There," said Mr Buffin, who was trying hard to think of some excuse for not getting up the ladder. But as he could think of none, he took his courage in both hands and said very quickly, "One, two, three, up!"

On the word "up", Mr Buffin said "One, two, three, up!" again because, although his courage was in both hands, his mind was not quite made up. It took a little time to make up his mind, and then after one more "One, two, three, up!" Mr Buffin started to climb. He climbed to the top. It was not as bad as he had thought, and after a short time he had tied most of the roses back against the wall.

It was while he was tying up the last of the roses that Harold Trotter came round the corner and saw the bottom of the ladder.

"Hullo, a brand new scratching place," he said to himself. And going as fast as he could, which was not very fast because he was so fat, he got behind the ladder and began to rub himself against it. It was delicious.

Mr Buffin felt the ladder moving.

"I knew I should feel giddy if I stayed up here," said Mr Buffin, clutching a rung of the ladder and shutting his eyes.

By now Harold Trotter was rubbing as hard as he could. Never had he had a better scratch. It was superb. The more he shoved and the more he pushed, the better it was.

But Harold Trotter went just a little too far. He rubbed and pushed and shoved and scratched so hard that he turned the ladder right over.

"Help, help!" shouted Mr Buffin, who had lost his grip and his balance, and was falling head foremost to the ground. But nothing could help Mr Buffin now. Even if there had been someone

there, he could have done nothing to save him. Mr Buffin was heading straight for the ground, and, sure enough, he hit it. Or, as Mr Buffin was inclined to think, it hit him. Mr Buffin saw a great many stars of different sizes and colours, and several things that looked like plates moving from left to right.

When Mr Buffin opened his eyes the stars and plates had gone and he saw Harold Trotter.

"So that was you, was it?" said Mr Buffin. "You wait until I've looked after myself, and then I'll attend to you."

Mr Buffin was not only hurt, he

was very angry, and he was all the more angry because besides being hurt he had been frightened. And there is nothing that is more likely to make one angry than being frightened.

Mr Buffin went into the house and put a bandage round his head. He wound several more yards of bandage than were strictly necessary, but as he had been hurt he meant to look it. And then he put some ointment round his eye, which was beginning to go black and blue and yellow. Altogether Mr Buffin felt very sorry for himself, and still more so when he looked in the glass, which he kept on doing throughout the day.

When he began to think about Harold Trotter, Mr Buffin thought long and seriously. Gradually Mr Buffin arrived at his decision. He decided that there was only one thing to do and that was to take Harold Trotter to market and sell him. Mr Buffin wanted to see no more of Harold Trotter. Mr Buffin was angry.

Meanwhile Harold Trotter was walking happily round the garden, scratching himself against this and against that, and having no idea at all that Mr Buffin had made such an important decision – a decision that was to be followed by such unpleasant results.

The next morning Mr Buffin got his car out of the garage. The car was rather an old-fashioned one. It was painted mauve and had brass lamps. Mr Buffin did not like motor cars, and that being so he saw no point in having an expensive new car.

With Harold Trotter on the seat beside him, Mr Buffin set out for market. Harold Trotter had no idea where he was going, and he sat on the seat with his ears pricked and thoroughly enjoyed the fresh air and the scenery.

The market was a long way off, and while the old car was puffing and panting along, Mr Buffin began to think.

If I sell Harold Trotter in the market, thought Mr Buffin, *he may go to the butcher's and be killed. He may be turned into sausages. And I wouldn't like that to happen*, thought Mr Buffin, *indeed I wouldn't.*

At this point of the journey the road ran through a deep, dark wood which was full of oak trees.

I know, thought Mr Buffin, *I'll leave Harold Trotter in this wood. He can live on the acorns and I need never be bothered with, or hurt by him again.* This struck Mr Buffin as a very good way out of the difficulty, and so he pushed Harold Trotter out of the car, turned the car round and started for home.

Harold Trotter felt very sad and lonely, as well as deserted and hungry. He had never been alone in a big wood before, and as he watched Mr Buffin drive away a large tear rolled down his cheek. In next to no time the car was so far away that Harold Trotter could no longer hear it. He was alone, all alone in the big dark wood. He ate some acorns.

Harold Trotter very soon found that acorns were no good. It took him a very long time to collect

enough to make a good mouthful; in fact it took him so long that he could not collect acorns fast enough to keep pace with his hunger. Harold Trotter knew that if he collected all the acorns in the wood he would still feel hungry. And in addition to this, he did not like acorns.

And so Harold Trotter made up his mind to go home. It would be a very, very long journey and would probably take him weeks, if not months, but Harold Trotter meant to go through with it. And Harold Trotter stamped each of his feet to show himself how determined he was.

Harold Trotter started off at once. He had a good sense of direction and knew that he would not lose the way. Being a very fat pig he soon became tired and often had to sit down for rests. But as the days went by he became thinner from having both so much exercise and so little to eat, and because he was thinner he was able to squeeze under gates and so to take short cuts.

Even so the journey took him a long time, during all of which he grew thinner and thinner, and more and more footsore. When at last he arrived at Mr Buffin's front door, he was a very thin pig indeed. He stood on the doorstep, looking up at the green door, and he had only just enough strength to give two feeble snorts.

For many days Mr Buffin had been worrying about Harold Trotter. Mr Buffin's head had healed and his eye was all right, and so he was beginning to think that he had been unkind to Harold Trotter. He was beginning to wonder how Harold Trotter was getting on, whether he was finding enough to eat and whether the nights were cold. Mr Buffin was in fact thinking of going to look for Harold Trotter when to his surprise he heard two feeble snorts.

"Can that be him?" wondered Mr Buffin. "No, of course it can't." But there came another two feeble snorts, and Mr Buffin went to the door. "My goodness, it is him," cried Mr Buffin, who was overjoyed to see Harold Trotter again.

Harold Trotter was very pleased to see Mr Buffin, and would have wagged his tail if it had not been screwed into such a tight twist.

Mr Buffin took Harold Trotter into the house and fed him on all the good things he could find. Harold Trotter soon began to recover and to put on weight. In fact, he became even fatter than he had been before, so fat, indeed, that he was only a short distance off the ground. However, that did not worry Harold Trotter. A pig is never happier than when he is really fat. There are many reasons for this, and one of this is that the fatter a pig is the more room he

217

has for scratching.

Harold Trotter went back to all his old scratching places and had a good rub, and now when the weather is fine and warm he is usually sure to find a pail of something good to eat beside Mr Buffin's garden chair.

The High Marmalade Cat

Fred Sedgwick

The high marmalade cat likes to sit on roofs.

She likes to sit on the roof of the nesting box in our garden, watching for blue tits. The blue tits fly in and out, but the high marmalade cat never catches them.

She thinks it's fun to sit on the roof of our house, to frighten the sparrows that stand on the chimneys. Then she looks down on everyone with a proud expression.

She even likes to sit on the roofs of houses where her friends live: the black cat, James; the black and white cat, Alice. She'll even sit on the roof of the fierce cat, Norman, who steals scraps from bins, and fights and squalls all night long.

And – I'm afraid – she likes to sit on the highest part of St Mary-le-Tower church.

She loves, if she can, to sit among the flags on the Queen's roof. Can you believe it? But she doesn't get up there very often.

And always, wherever she sits,

people say: "Look! There's the marmalade cat, sitting up there."

When she feels like it, she comes down, however high the roof, one paw after another, carefully, creeping down and down until, at last, she leaps the last bit – *jump* – and lands safe on the ground.

Then she wonders where her tea

might be, and where she might get a cuddle.

Oh yes, the marmalade cat likes to sit on roofs.

On Sunday last week, she climbed onto one that was very high.

It wasn't the roof of the nesting box. It wasn't the roof of our house, nor one of the roofs of houses where her friends live. Not James's roof, nor Alice's, nor Norman's. It wasn't another roof she liked, the one on St Mary-le-Tower church. It wasn't the Queen's roof.

It was the highest roof of the airport. We could see the cat up there against the sky, looking around as the aeroplanes roared in and out.

I called my wife's rabbit, but she couldn't get the cat down.

I called my son Daniel's guinea pig Eric, but he couldn't get the cat down.

I called the vicar's tortoise, but she couldn't get the cat down.

My wife's rabbit, Daniel's guinea pig Eric, and the vicar's tortoise looked up at the high marmalade cat.

I called my big friendly dog Jessie, but she couldn't get the cat down. I called my hamster, but she couldn't get the cat down.

I called my goldfish, but – no, he

couldn't get the cat down.

My wife's rabbit, Daniel's guinea pig Eric, the vicar's tortoise, my friendly dog Jessie, my hamster and my goldfish all looked up at the high marmalade cat.

I called my favourite horse, but he couldn't get the cat down.

I called my uncle's sheep, but they couldn't get the cat down.

I called for the lovely cow my father has in his field, but – no, she couldn't get the cat down.

My wife's rabbit, Daniel's guinea pig Eric, the vicar's tortoise, my friendly dog Jessie, my hamster, my goldfish, my favourite horse, my uncle's sheep and the lovely

cow my father has in his field all looked up at the high marmalade cat.

I called for the Prime Minister's goat (he's called Samuel, I think), but he couldn't get the cat down.

I called for the Queen's fiercest corgi (Dawn? Jacquie? Henrietta?

– I can't remember her name), but she couldn't get the cat down.

Even *I* tried to get the cat down, and I am middle-aged and tubby, and I gave up climbing many years ago.

My wife's rabbit, Daniel's guinea pig Eric, the vicar's tortoise, my friendly dog Jessie, my hamster, my goldfish, my favourite horse, my uncle's sheep, the lovely cow my father has in his field, the Prime Minister's goat (I'm almost certain he's called Samuel), the Queen's fiercest corgi (Dawn? Jacquie? Henrietta? – I can't remember her name) and I (who am middle-aged and tubby, and who gave up climbing many years ago) all looked up at the high marmalade cat.

Then my son Daniel said, "Look! Look!"

And the high marmalade cat came down.

She came down, one paw after another, carefully, creeping down and down over flat roofs, shiny roofs, sloped roofs, glass roofs, steep roofs until, at last, she leapt the last bit – *jump* – and landed safely on the ground.

Then she came to Daniel for a cuddle, and back to our house for tea.

ACKNOWLEDGEMENTS

The publishers wish to thank the following for permission to reproduce copyright material:

Naomi Adler: "Never Trust a Pelican" from *Barefoot Book of Animal Tales*; first published by Barefoot Books 1996 and reproduced with their permission.

Anne English: "How the Animals Got Tails" from *Animal Stories* compiled by Julia Eccleshare; first published by Orchard Books 1992 and reproduced with their permission.

Linda Greenbury: "Pussy Simkin meets a Peacock Bird" from *Pussy Simkin* by Linda Greenbury; first published by BBC Books 1969 and reproduced with their permission.

Meredith Hooper: "Alpha Beta and Grandma Delta" from *A Puffin Bedtime Story Chest* compiled by Barbara Ireson; first published by Penguin Books and © Meredith Hooper 1986; reproduced by permission of David Higham Associates on behalf of the author.

Annette Elizabeth Clark: "The Tale of Brave Augustus" from *Country Tales* by Annette Elizabeth Clark; first published by Hodder & Stoughton 1996 and reproduced with their permission.

Margaret Mahy: "A Lion in the Meadow" from *A Lion in the Meadow* by Margaret Mahy; first published by Orion Children's Books 1976 and reproduced with their permission.

David Henry Wilson: "Eight Hairy Legs" from *How to Stop a Train with One Finger* by David Henry Wilson; first published by Orion Children's Books 1984 and reproduced with their permission.

Andrew Matthews: "The Rat Wedding" from *The Beasts of Boggart Hollow* by Andrew Matthews; first published by Orion Children's Books 1996 and reproduced with their permission.

Sheila Lavelle: "Ursula on the Farm" from *Ursula on the Farm* by Sheila Lavelle; © Sheila Lavelle 1987; first published by Hamish Hamilton Children's Books 1987 and reproduced with their permission.

Ann and Reg Cartwright: "The Winter Hedgehog"; first published by

ACKNOWLEDGEMENTS

Hutchinson/Red Fox 1989 and reproduced by permission of Random House UK Ltd.

Anita Hewett: "Koala's Walkabout" from *The Anita Hewett Animal Story Book* by Anita Hewett; first published by Bodley Head 1972 and reproduced by permission of Random House UK Ltd.

Dorothy Edwards: "The Miserable Mouse" from *The Old Man Who Sneezed* by Dorothy Edwards; first published by Methuen Children's Books 1983 and reproduced by permission of Rogers, Coleridge & White Ltd on behalf of the author.

Fred Sedgwick: "The High Marmalade Cat" from *Animal Stories*; first published by Simon & Schuster Young Books 1994 and reproduced with their permission.

Hazel Townson: "Snake on the Bus" from *Snake on the Bus and Other Pet Stories*; first published by Methuen Children's Books 1994 and reproduced with their permission.

Dick King-Smith: "The Excitement of Being Ernest" from *A Narrow Squeak and Other Animal Stories* 1993; reproduced by permission of A.P. Watt on behalf of Fox Busters Ltd for Dick King-Smith.

Every effort has been made to trace the copyright holders but where this has not been possible or where any error has been made the publishers will be pleased to make the necessary arrangement at the first opportunity.

Funny stories

for 6 year olds

Chosen by Helen Paiba

A bright and varied selection of wonderfully
entertaining stories by some of the very
best writers for children. Perfect for
reading alone or aloud – and for dipping
into time and time again. With stories from
Margaret Mahy, David Henry Wilson, Francesca
Simon, Tony Bradman and many more,
this book will provide hours of fantastic fun.

Funny stories

for 7 Year Olds

Chosen by Helen Paiba

A bright and varied selection of wonderfully
entertaining stories by some of the very
best writers for children. Perfect for reading
alone or aloud – and for dipping into time
and time again. With stories from Dick
King-Smith, Michael Bond, Philippa Gregory,
Jacqueline Wilson and many more,
this book will provide hours of fantastic fun.

Funny Stories

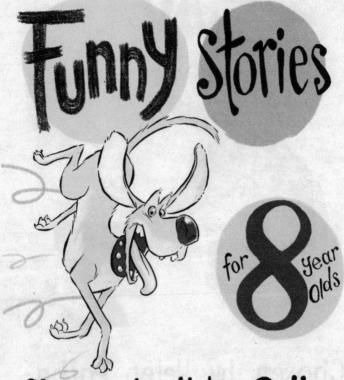

for **8** year olds

Chosen by Helen Paiba

A bright and varied selection of wonderfully entertaining stories by some of the very best writers for children. Perfect for reading alone or aloud – and for dipping into time and time again. With stories from Judy Blume, Anne Fine, Dick King-Smith, Morris Gleitzman and many more, this book will provide hours of fantastic fun.